· T R O P H I E S ·

Intervention
PRACTICE BOOK
Grade 2

Harcourt

Orlando   Boston   Dallas   Chicago   San Diego

Visit *The Learning Site!*
www.harcourtschool.com

Printed in the United States of America

ISBN 0-15-326150-1

3 4 5 6 7 8 9 10 054 10 09 08 07 06 05 04 03 02

Table of Contents

Fluency Builder

dull	things	Mac
exciting	see	animals
handsome	look	wap
hardly	wait	zap
sideways		fan
sparkling		that
spotted		had
		sad
		bad

1. Mac thought / things were dull.

2. He wanted to go / to the zoo / to see the exciting animals.

3. Mac saw / two spotted / and handsome animals / at the zoo.

4. They could look sideways / with their long necks.

5. Mac wished / he could look / like the animal / that had a sparkling fan.

6. Wap! / Zap! / Mac's wish / came true.

7. Mac could hardly wait / to show his pals / how handsome he was.

8. Mac was sad / and felt bad / when he had no pals.

Harcourt

Mac's Wish Comes True

Write the word from the box that best completes each sentence.

| cat | pan | bat | van | hat | sad |

1. My _____ cat _____ is in my lap.

2. The jam is in the _____ pan _____ .

3. Pam has on a _____ hat _____ .

4. This man is not _____ sad _____ .

5. That _____ bat _____ had a nap.

6. A cat is in that _____ van _____ !

Harcourt

Mac's Wish Comes True

Complete the flowchart with words from the box to tell what happens in "Mac's Wish Comes True."

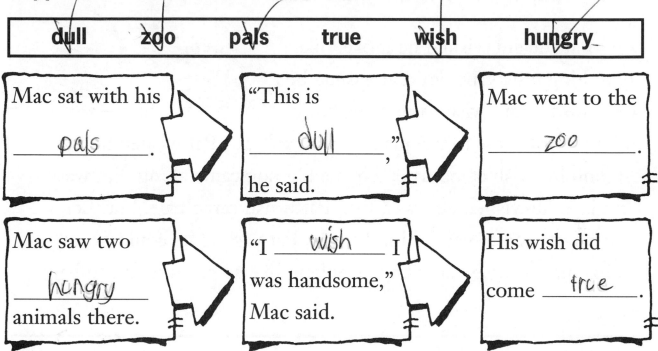

| dull | zoo | pals | true | wish | hungry |

Mac sat with his _____pals_____.

"This is _____dull_____," he said.

Mac went to the _____zoo_____.

Mac saw two _____hungry_____ animals there.

"I _____wish_____ I was handsome," Mac said.

His wish did come _____true_____.

Write the answers to these questions to tell the rest of the story.

1. What did Mac wish for next? _to be sparkling_____

_____

2. What did the animals in the river ask Mac when he got home?

_Who are you?_____

3. What did you like best in this story?

_Responses will vary._____

_____

Harcourt

Main Idea

Write three clues that tell about the main idea of the paragraph. Then write the main idea.

Pat the ant wished he looked like something else. One day Pat wished he was a bird. Pat's wish came true, but he did not know how to use his new wings. Next, Pat wished he was a cat, and his wish came true. Then a big dog came along. Pat was afraid, so he wished he was a fish. Pat's wish came true, but then a fisherman tried to catch him. Finally, Pat wished he could be an ant again, and his wish came true. Looking like an ant was not so bad!

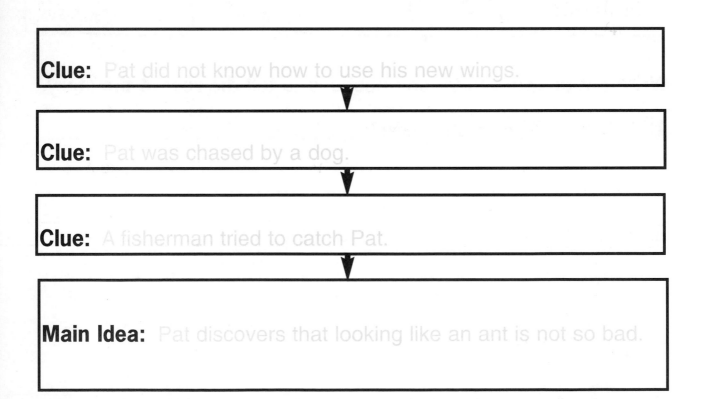

Clue: Pat did not know how to use his new wings.

Clue: Pat was chased by a dog.

Clue: A fisherman tried to catch Pat.

Main Idea: Pat discovers that looking like an ant is not so bad.

Harcourt

Name **Ryan**

Fluency Builder

always	get	Stan
homework	does	Fran
minutes	must	stands
snuggle	what	add
treat	coming	black
	company	grab
	trip	glad
		Brad

1. Fran always / does her homework, / while Brad / eats a treat.

2. Fran wants / to add black / to her map.

3. In just ten minutes, / Stan must / get off the mat.

4. Cass wants to snuggle /with her cat, / but there is no more time.

5. Dad tells the children / to stop / what they are doing.

6. Stan is glad / that company is coming, / but Dad is the one / that has to grab / all the toys.

7. Dad picks up / all the toys / so that the company / will not trip / on them.

8. In the end, / the family stands together / to wait / for their company.

Name Ryan

Company Is Coming!

Read the story. Circle all the words that begin with two consonants.

Stan has a cat and a flag. Fran has a hat. Stan and Fran skip.

Stan trips. He drops his cat and his flag. Fran has a plan.

Fran grabs her hat. Fran grabs his cat. Fran grabs his flag.

Stan is glad. His cat is glad. Stan and his cat like Fran.

Write the word that best completes each sentence.

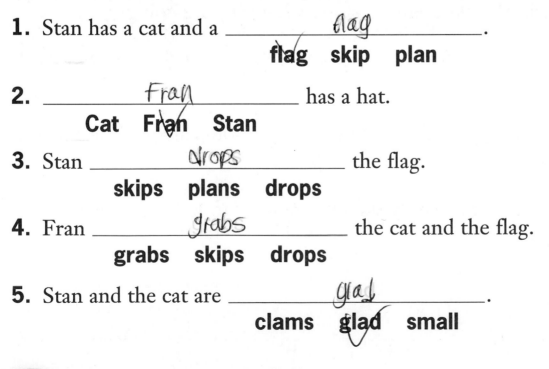

1. Stan has a cat and a _____ flag _____.

   flag   skip   plan

2. _____ Fran _____ has a hat.

   Cat   Fran   Stan

3. Stan _____ drops _____ the flag.

   skips   plans   drops

4. Fran _____ grabs _____ the cat and the flag.

   grabs   skips   drops

5. Stan and the cat are _____ glad _____.

   clams   glad   small

Harcourt

Company Is Coming!

Read the story. Then fill in the chart with details about the family.

Dad wanted everyone to get ready because company was coming to visit. Little Brad was not ready because he was eating a treat. Fran was not ready because she was doing her homework. Cass was not ready because she was playing with the cat. Stan was not ready because he was on the mat. Finally, everyone was ready, but then Dad was missing. He was taking a nap just when company came to the door.

Why isn't Brad ready?	Why isn't Fran ready?
He is eating a treat.	She is doing her homework.
He is eating a treat	She is doin her homework
Why isn't Cass ready?	**Why isn't Stan ready?**
She is playing with the cat.	He is on the mat.
She is play Tng with the cat	He ison th mat

Author's Purpose

Write the author's purpose. Then write three clues that helped you tell the author's purpose.

Company was coming to Fred Frog's house. "Get ready," Fred Frog called to his froggy brothers. "Company is coming in ten minutes!"

None of Fred Frog's froggy brothers were ready. They were all busy playing baseball, sailing boats, and eating pizza. "Please help me clean up all these lily pads!" called Fred Frog. "Company is coming in five minutes!"

Author's Purpose: to entertain

Clue: The story is made up.

Clue: Frogs can't talk, play baseball, sail boats, or eat pizza.

Clue: Frogs don't have company or clean up their lily pads.

Harcourt

Fluency Builder

chipmunks	down	Kim
picked	fall	Tip
sniffing	few	bit
south	apples	did
woods	trees	will
	could	zip
	go	sit
	were	

1. Kim and Tip / loved to go / for walks / in the woods.

2. Kim / loved walking / in the fall leaves.

3. Tip loved / sniffing the fall leaves.

4. Kim picked / a few apples, / and her dog / looked for chipmunks.

5. The apple trees / were south / of the woods.

6. Kim and Tip / will sit / for a bit.

7. They will see / a chipmunk / zip up the tree.

8. They could see / the chipmunk, / but it did not / come down.

the chipmunks picked apples.
could Kim go up trees

Harcourt

Name _Ryan_

A Walk in the Woods

Fill in the oval in front of the sentence that tells about the picture.

1
- ⬭ My cat hid in the tin.
- ⬭ Tim did find his bat.
- ⬤ The cat sits in his lap.

✓

2
- ⬭ She is sitting with her bat.
- ⬭ She is sitting in a van.
- ⬤ She is hitting now.

✓

3
- ⬭ Is that a pig in the van?
- ⬭ That pig is so big!
- ⬤ I see a pig in a wig.

✓

4
- ⬭ Tim finds a pin in the bin.
- ⬭ Is the wig in the bin?
- ⬤ All my hats are in the bin.

✓

5
- ⬭ She did win a bat.
- ⬤ She did win a pin.
- ⬭ She is in the van.

✓

6
- ⬭ This fits him.
- ⬤ This is big for him.
- ⬭ He is sitting down.

✓

Harcourt

Name _Karen Ryan_

A Walk in the Woods

Complete the story strip to show what happened in "A Walk in the Woods."

When do Kim and Tip like to go for walks? _In the fall_ fall	Where do Kim and Tip like to go for walks? in the woods woods
Who loves sniffing the leaves? Tip Tip	Who loves the apples in the trees? Kim Kim
What animal do Kim and Tip see? a chipmunk Chipmunk	What if you could go for a walk in the woods. What would you like to see there? Responses will vary. Birds

Harcourt

Name Ryan

Narrative Elements (Setting)

Write the setting of the paragraph. Write two clues that tell when and two clues that tell where.

   One hundred years ago, a boy named Max lived in a treehouse in a very tall tree. The very tall tree grew in a forest called Big Green Forest. One summer day, Max's dog, Kip, woke him up. Max and Kip heard a funny sound coming from the roof of the treehouse.

Setting: in a treehouse in the Big Green Forest, one hundred years ago, on a summer day	
Clue That Tells When: one hundred years ago	**Clue That Tells When:** one summer day
Clue That Tells Where: in a treehouse in a very tall tree	**Clue That Tells Where:** in a forest called Big Green Forest

Harcourt

Fluency Builder

alone	**fun**	**call**
cheer	**right**	**all**
fine	**made**	**wall**
meadow	**think**	**tall**
reason	**play**	**mall**
spoiled	**when**	**ball**
	friends	**fine**

1. Hal sat / alone at home, / but he did not think / it was fun.

2. He made a call, / and asked Rip / to cheer him up.

3. Rip's nap / was spoiled, / but he felt / all right.

4. Mack is digging / in the meadow / when Hal calls.

5. Hal / had no reason / to be alone.

6. The friends / could all / play ball.

7. It was a fine day / to go to the river, / or visit the mall.

8. Hal sat / next to the tall wall / as he made his call.

One Fine Night

Write the word that makes the sentence tell about the picture.

1. It is _____ fall _____.

       fall   **fan**   **for**

2. Kim and her dad are at the

_____ mall _____.

    make   **mall**   **man**

3. They go down a big _____ hall _____.

        pal   **have**   **hall**

4. "Look over this _____ wall _____, Kim."

      will   **wall**   **wax**

5. Kim is not _____ tall _____.

      tall   **that**   **tap**

6. "Look at _____ all _____ the cats!"

      are   **and**   **all**

7. "Can I have the one with the _____ ball _____?"

      ban   **bat**   **ball**

8. "We will _____ call _____ Mom."

    come   **call**   **can**

Harcourt

Name _____

One Fine Night

Fill in the story map to tell about "One Fine Night." Use the words in the gray boxes. Possible responses are shown.

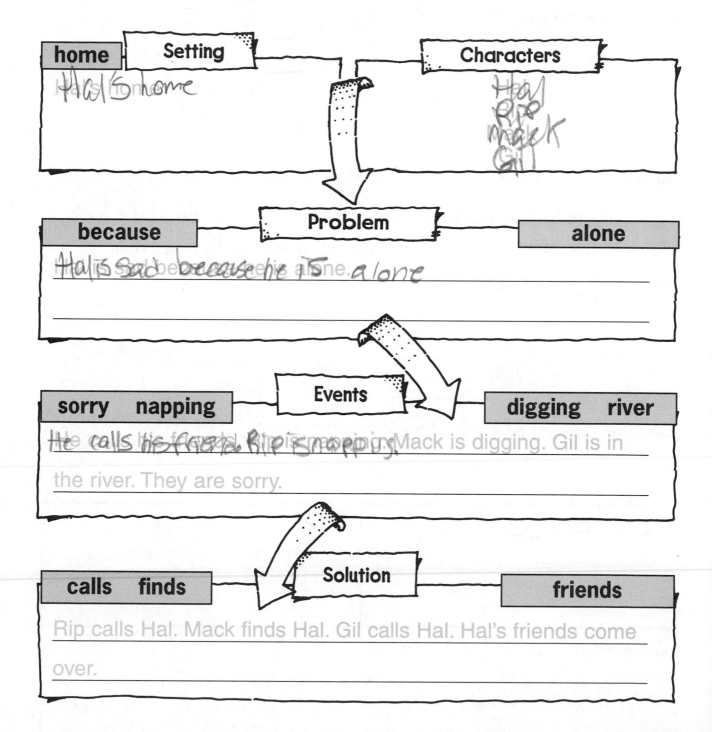

Setting | home
Hal's home

Characters
Hal
Rip
Mack
Gil

Problem | because | alone
Hal is sad because he is alone.

Events | sorry napping | digging river
He calls his friends. Rip is napping. Mack is digging. Gil is in the river. They are sorry.

Solution | calls finds | friends
Rip calls Hal. Mack finds Hal. Gil calls Hal. Hal's friends come over.

Harcourt

Selection Comprehension/Lesson 4 • Grade 2 **17**

Compare and Contrast

Read the two stories. Compare and contrast the characters.

Pal's Fine Night

Pal sits in his dog house. He is happy being alone. It is a very fine night to look at the stars and think about how lucky he is to be a dog. Pal is very glad that he has such a big dog house.

Sal's Lonely Night

Sal sits in his dog house. He is lonely. He is afraid of the dark. He does not like to look at the stars. Sal is sad in his dog house because it is too small.

Characters: Pal and Sal	**Alike:** both are dogs, both are sitting in their dog houses at night one summer day
Different: Pal likes to be alone and look at the stars; he has a big dog house. Sal is lonely and does not like to look at the stars; he has a small dog house.	

Harcourt

Name _____

Fluency Builder

amazing	ball	Bob
clustered	but	pot
gathered	snow	mop
raced	watch	hop
wandered	look	hot
	friend	not
	groups	
	one	
	after	

1. The children clustered / in groups, / but I did not.

2. I gathered snow / and made one ball / after another.

3. Bob / was amazing, / but he could not / get hot.

4. Each time / I raced, / Bob would / watch me.

5. I wandered alone / to look / for a pot / and a mop.

6. Bob would watch / me hop.

7. A snow friend / cannot be there / when it is hot.

8. Do you want / to know / the name / of my snow friend?

Harcourt

Just You and Me

Read the story. Circle all the words with the short *o* vowel sound.

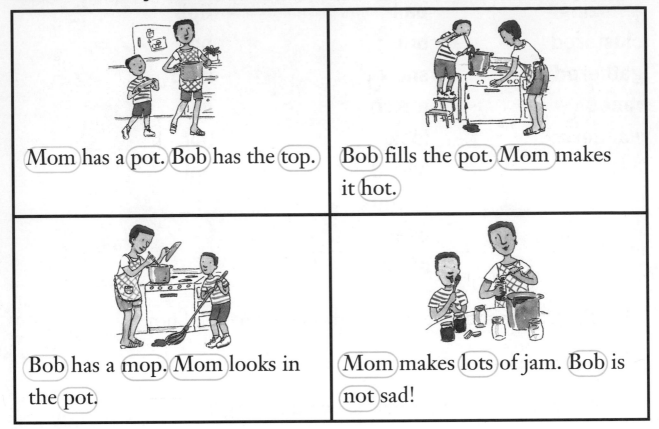

Mom has a pot. Bob has the top. | Bob fills the pot. Mom makes it hot.

Bob has a mop. Mom looks in the pot. | Mom makes lots of jam. Bob is not sad!

Circle the word to complete each sentence. Write it on the line.

1. Mom got the _____pot_____.

       pit   **pot**   pat

2. Bob got a _____top_____ for the pot.

      tap   tip   **top**

3. Mom made the pot _____hot_____.

      hit   hat   **hot**

4. Bob had to get the _____mop_____.

      mop   man   mad

5. Bob likes jam a _____lot_____!

      lid   lap   **lot**

Harcourt

Just You and Me

Write *beginning,* *middle,* **or** *end* **to show when each thing happened.**

_____middle_____   _____end_____   _____beginning_____

Now write what happened in the story. Use the words in the boxes in your answers. Possible responses are shown.

Beginning: | school   played   friends |

The boy had no friends at school. The friends all played together.

Middle: | snow   loved   Bob |

The boy made a snow friend named Bob. The friends loved Bob.

End: | friends   desk |

Now the boy sits at his desk with his new friends.

Harcourt

Narrative Elements (Character)

**Read the story. Fill in the chart with a character. Then write
clues from the story that tell about the character.**

Mara's Play Pal

Mara sat alone on her front steps and watched the other children
play. Everyone had a play pal except her. All of a sudden, a little white
cat came to sit next to her. "I am lonely, little kitty," said Mara. "Will
you play with me?" The cat rubbed against Mara's arm and purred.
Mara smiled. For the rest of the day, Mara played with the cat.

Character:	**Word Clues:**
Mara	"I am lonely."

Action Clues: Mara sat alone and watched the other children play; Mara smiled; Mara played with the cat.

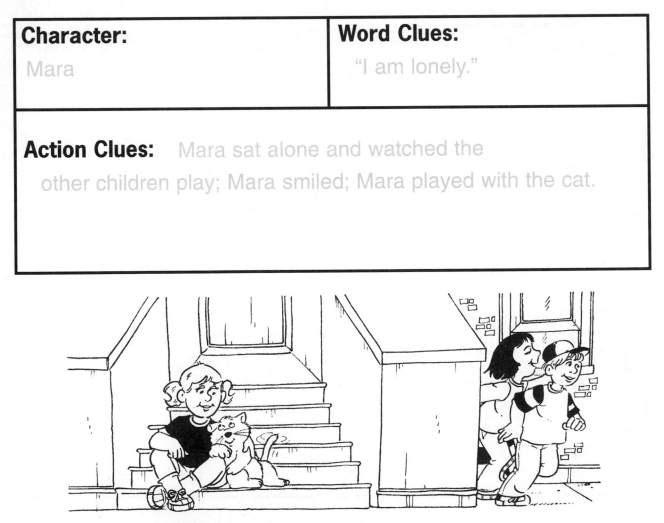

Harcourt

Fluency Builder

enormous	hill	get
granddaughter	some	men
grew	help	fell
planted	well	best
strong	mouse	then
turnip	woman	bent
		rest
		mess

1. A woman / planted a turnip / on a hill.

2. The turnip / grew to be / enormous.

3. The turnip / fell into the well / and made a mess.

4. The woman / called / her granddaughter / to help.

5. They pulled, / but they could not get / the turnip / out of the well.

6. Some strong men / came to help, / but they could not pull / the turnip / from the well.

7. Then / a mouse said, / "I can help."

8. The mouse / bent over / the well / and did his best.

9. The rest helped, / and they pulled / the turnip / out at last.

A Turnip's Tale

Write the word that best completes each sentence.

wet	nest	bell	ten	bed	sled	men

1. Two _____ men _____ go to the zoo.

2. The cat is on the _____ bed _____ .

3. Can you see the _____ bell _____ ?

4. Her _____ sled _____ can go down.

5. The _____ nest _____ is in the tree.

6. These animals are _____ wet _____ .

7. There are _____ ten _____ red apples.

Harcourt

A Turnip's Tale

**These events are from "A Turnip's Tale." They are out of order.
Write a number in front of each one to show the right order.**

__5__ A mouse came to help.

__3__ The granddaughter asked
some men to help.

__1__ The turnip fell into a well.

__4__ They all pulled, but they
could not get the turnip out.

__2__ The woman called her granddaughter.

**Now write each event in the order it happened. Put each one
next to an X. Then write other story events on the blank lines.**

[X] The turnip fell into a well.

[X] The woman called her granddaughter.

[X] The granddaughter asked some men to help.

[X] They all pulled, but they could not get the turnip out.

[X] A mouse came to help.

Possible response: The mouse showed the people how to

pour water into the well so the turnip would come up.

Then they pulled the turnip out. Everyone was glad.

Harcourt

Sequence

These sentences are not in time order.

The carrot grew to be enormous.

After it grew, the enormous carrot rolled down the hill.

First, an old woman planted a carrot on a hill.

Finally, the carrot rolled into the pond.

Write the sentences in correct order to complete the diagram.

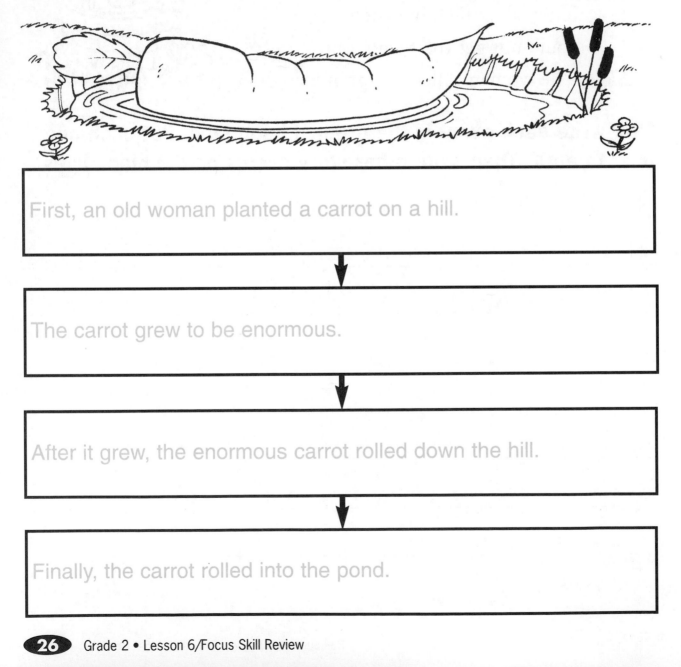

First, an old woman planted a carrot on a hill.

The carrot grew to be enormous.

After it grew, the enormous carrot rolled down the hill.

Finally, the carrot rolled into the pond.

Harcourt

Fluency Builder

alongside	used	wish
chores	what	dishes
engine	fix	Tish
simple	help	Shep
sprout	flowers	brush
tool	thinks	wash
	paint	shop

1. Ted likes digging / with a tool / alongside his mom.

2. Ted makes a wish / that the plants / will sprout / pretty flowers.

3. Doing the dishes / is Jim's chore.

4. Jim thinks / it is simple / to wash the plates.

5. Tish helps / her dad / fix an engine / in the shop.

6. Ben used / a paint brush / to help paint / the fence.

7. Pat thinks / walking Shep / is like playing.

8. What chores / do you do?

Tools That Help

Fill in the oval in front of the sentence that tells about the picture.

1. ⬭ Ben hands her his cash.
   ⬭ Ben makes a dash to the shed.
   ⬭ Ben makes a wish.

2. ⬭ Tad looks at the big ship.
   ⬭ Tad has a pet fish.
   ⬭ Tad has lost his dish.

3. ⬭ Jen drops the dish.
   ⬭ Jen sees a red fish.
   ⬭ Jen is on a ship.

4. ⬭ The shed fell over.
   ⬭ I see a hen on the ship.
   ⬭ The hen is in the shed.

5. ⬭ The cat has a fish.
   ⬭ The cat sits by the shop.
   ⬭ Now a cat is in the shack!

6. ⬭ They wish they had a ball and bat.
   ⬭ They find a shell.
   ⬭ They make a dash for the bus.

Harcourt

Name **Ryan**

Tools That Help

Complete the puzzle by using words from the box.

digging	learning	job	paid	helping	tools	chore

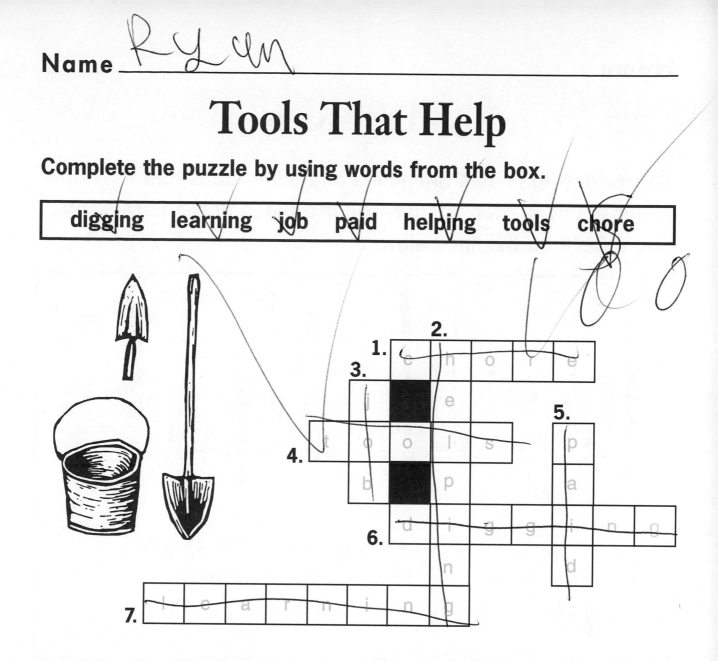

Across

1. Pat's _____ is walking her dog.

4. Some kids used _____ to help with the jobs.

6. Ted likes _____ with his mom.

7. Tish is _____ as she works.

Down

2. Jim likes _____ out at home.

3. Tish said that fixing an engine is a _____ for an adult.

5. Jim is not _____ for washing the dishes.

Harcourt

Main Idea

This paragraph has a main idea and other ideas that tell more about the main idea. Identify the main idea of the paragraph, and write it on the line below.

Leah likes to clean the garage. First, she wipes off the garden tools. Then, she puts them away. The last thing she does is sweep the floor.

Main Idea ___Leah likes to clean the garage_____

_____

Harcourt

Fluency Builder

cranes	this	Lun
directions	here	Crump
promise	some	dug
twitch	toy	but
worry	shop	Bud
		Muffin
		sun
		hum
		bug
		rug

1. "Mr. Crump, / will that plane / run?" / asked Lun.

2. "No, / but this / plane will," / said Mr. Crump.

3. "Here are / the directions," / said Mr. Crump.

4. Bud looked / at some cranes / in the toy shop.

5. Mr. Crump's cat, / Muffin, / was sitting / in the sun.

6. Muffin twitched / when she heard / the hum / of a bug.

7. Muffin dug / in the rug / for the bug.

8. Mr. Crump said, / "Do not worry, / because I promise / that Muffin will get the bug."

The Promise

Read the sentences. Look at the picture. Then do what the sentences tell you.

1. Ned has a jug. Make it red.

2. Draw a cup for Ned.

3. Find the plums. Draw an apple to go with the plums.

4. Draw the sun over the trees.

5. Draw a red bug on a tree.

6. A pup runs to Ned. Make it black.

7. Find the animal that likes nuts. Draw some nuts for it.

Now circle the words in the sentences that have the short _u_ sound.

Harcourt

The Promise

Read the sentences. Choose and write the word to complete each one. Use the words to retell the first part of the story.

1. Lun asks Mr. Crump if the _____plane_____ **bug plane cat** will go.	**2.** Lun and his mom _____bought_____ **lost bent bought** the toy.
3. Bud asks Mr. Crump if the crane will _____start_____. **start lift stop**	**4.** Muffin is Mr. Crump's _____cat_____. **bug toy cat**

Use words from the box to answer these questions. Write your answers on the lines to retell the rest of the story.

toys   bug   fly

5. What did Bud's dad say a bug can do? _____fly_____

6. What spilled over in the shop when Muffin jumped at the

bug? _____toys_____

7. What did Muffin see at the end of the story? _____bug_____

Predict Outcomes

The ending of this paragraph is missing. Look for clues. Then predict what will happen next.

> Mr. Tibbit fell asleep in the chair. His cat, Blackie, sat in his lap. Suddenly, Mr. Tibbit let out a loud snore. Blackie jerked and fell out of the chair. He woke up Mr. Tibbit. Blackie crawled back in Mr. Tibbit's lap. Mr. Tibbit fell asleep. Suddenly, Mr. Tibbit let out a loud snore. _____.

Write the clues you used to make your prediction. Draw a picture to show what you predict will happen next.

Clues	Predicted Outcome
Mr. Tibbit let out a loud snore.	Responses will vary.
Blackie jerked and fell out of the chair.	
He woke up Mr. Tibbit.	

Harcourt

Fluency Builder

batter	went	think
buttery	cake	whiz
perfect	put	thud
recipe	smell	thump
smeared	fell	wham
yellow cake	began	what
		bathtub
		thick

1. Possum said, / "I think cupcakes / are grand."

2. Rabbit / was a whiz / in the kitchen.

3. He had a recipe / for a buttery / yellow cake.

4. Possum dropped the bowl, / and it went thud, / thump, / and wham!

5. "What can we put / our cake batter in now?" / asked Possum.

6. Rabbit said, / "It will be perfect / to put / the thick batter / into the bathtub."

7. Possum fell in the tub / and was smeared / with batter.

8. Rabbit put / the cupcakes / into the open oven, / and soon the kitchen / began to smell good.

Too Many Cupcakes

Read the story. Circle all the words with *wh* or *th*.

Seth Makes Broth

(Seth) makes (broth.) He wants his (broth) to be (thick.) Now (Seth) has some (broth.) It is not (thick.) It is (thin!)

(Seth) (whips) up an egg. He adds the egg to his (broth.) Now his (broth) is (thick.) (Seth) is glad.

Circle and write the word that best completes each sentence.

1. Seth makes _____ broth _____.

      whip (**broth**) **path**

2. Seth likes _____ thick _____ broth.

      bath **when** (**thick**)

3. The broth Seth makes is _____ thin _____.

      tin (**thin**) **with**

4. Seth _____ whips _____ an egg.

      (**whips**) **with** **wishes**

5. Now the broth is _____ thick _____.

      (**thick**) **both** **when**

Name _____

Too Many Cupcakes

Answer the questions below to tell about "Too Many Cupcakes."

1. Who was a whiz in the kitchen, Possum or Rabbit?

Rabbit

2. Who let the bowl land with a crash?

Possum

3. What did Rabbit and Possum mix in the bathtub?

batter

4. Who fell into the bathtub?

Possum

5. How did the hot oven help Possum?

It cooked the batter

on Possum.

6. What can Possum do with the cupcakes?

Eat them.

What do you like best in the story?

Responses will vary.

Harcourt

Synonyms

Read each sentence. Find the synonym for the underlined word. Write it on the line above the underlined word.

_____ house _____

1. Robin was building a new <u>home</u> in the apple tree.

   school   house   library

_____ sticks _____

2. Robin used many small <u>twigs</u> to make a nest.

   sticks   stones   nuts

_____ keep _____

3. "What can I use to <u>hold</u> the twigs together?" Robin wondered.

   move   keep   push

Reread each sentence with your word choice to make sure the sentence makes sense.

Harcourt

Fluency Builder

announced	some	Barb
arrived	enough	yard
glum	fell	Mark
members	idea	Karl
rebuild	number	started
	because	card
	stand	are
	said	

1. Barb / was glum / because she missed / her friends.

2. She took / some lemonade / to the kids / in the next yard.

3. Their clubhouse fell down, / and they didn't have / enough money / to rebuild it.

4. Karl had the idea / to sell lemonade / to earn money.

5. A large number / of people arrived / to buy lemonade.

6. When they closed the stand, / Mark announced / that they had enough money.

7. A card / on the clubhouse door / said / "Just Members."

8. Barb started to leave, / but Karl said, / "You are a friend, / and that makes you a member."

Harcourt

A Lemonade Surprise

Circle the word that makes the sentence tell about the picture.
Then write the word.

1. "It is time to go. Let's get into the

_____car_____ ," said Mom.

barn (**car**) **cat**

2. We got a snack at the

_____market_____ .

farm **barn** (**market**)

3. It was not _____far_____

(**far**) **yard** **fat**

to the park.

4. I got up on the _____bars_____ .

(**bars**) **jars** **harm**

5. It was _____hard_____

had (**hard**) **tar**

to find Mark when he hid.

6. We left the park when it got

_____dark_____ .

wet (**dark**) **cart**

7. We had fun at the _____park_____ !

(**park**) **farm** **pack**

Harcourt

A Lemonade Surprise

Read the clues. Then complete the puzzle with words from the box.

| clubhouse | empty | sales | wrong | money |

Across

2. Many people bought lemonade, so _____ were good.

4. When Barb was sad, her mom asked, "What's _____?"

5. At last, the lemonade jug was _____.

Down

1. The kids wanted to rebuild the _____.

3. Barb added up the _____.

Puzzle grid:

1. down: c l u b h o u s e

2. across: s a l e s

3. down: m o n e y

4. across: w r o n g

5. across: e m p t y

Write what you liked best about the story. Use as many words from the box as you can.

Responses will vary.

_____

_____

_____

_____

Harcourt

Compare and Contrast

Read the stories.

My Family's Vacation	Our Trip to the East
My family went on vacation out West. We saw mountains. We saw the desert. We went swimming in the ocean.	My family went east on vacation. We saw mountains. We saw the forest. We went swimming in the ocean.

In the middle part of the diagram, write what is the same in the two stories. In the outside parts, write what is different.

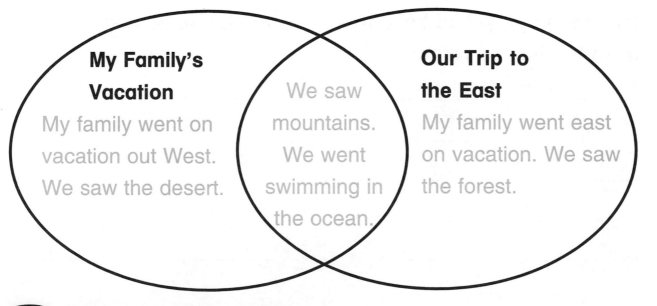

My Family's Vacation
My family went on vacation out West. We saw the desert.

We saw mountains. We went swimming in the ocean.

Our Trip to the East
My family went east on vacation. We saw the forest.

Harcourt

Fluency Builder

frontier	down	batch
nearby	fish	Charles
orchards	country	ditch
survive	must	chop
tame	rain	catch
wild	tree	watch
		stitch
		Mitch

1. You must tame / a wild animal / to survive / on the frontier.

2. Mitch / can catch fish / in the rain.

3. Anna / will pick apples / in the orchard nearby.

4. Anna / likes / the country.

5. Charles /will chop down / a tree.

6. Garth picks / a batch of apples / and puts them / in a basket.

7. Watch out / so you don't fall / into the ditch!

8. Mom will stitch the dress / before going / to sleep.

Name_____

Anna's Apple Doll

Fill in the oval in front of the sentence that tells about the picture.

1 ⬭ The chick has an itch on its chest.
   ⬬ The cat has an itch on its chin.
   ⬭ The cat has an itch on its back.

2 ⬬ Dan can stitch the patch.
   ⬭ Dan can catch a fast pitch.
   ⬭ We will switch the chart.

3 ⬭ Mitch is catching a fish.
   ⬭ Anna can pitch fast.
   ⬬ Anna is catching that ball.

4 ⬭ Ben and Sam chat by the ditch.
   ⬭ Ben and Sam pitch in the kitchen.
   ⬬ Ben and Sam chat in the kitchen.

5 ⬭ Chen and Pat have matching patches.
   ⬭ Chen and Pat have matching charms.
   ⬬ Chen and Pat have matching charts.

6 ⬭ Mitch is stitching a patch.
   ⬭ Mitch is catching a pitch.
   ⬬ Mitch is switching his hat.

Name _____

Anna's Apple Doll

Think about what happened in "Anna's Apple Doll."
Write about the *beginning*, *middle*, and *end* of the
play. Use the words from the boxes in your answers.

Beginning   `cabin   west`

Where does the play happen?

Possible response: The play happens in a cabin in the west.

_____

What does Anna's mom ask her to do?   `outdoors   apples`

Possible response: She asks her to go outdoors

to get a big batch of apples.

Middle   `seeds   sticks`

What does Anna use to make her doll?

Possible response: Anna uses seeds and sticks.

_____

End   `cabin   family`

Where does Anna take her doll? What happens there?

Possible response: Anna takes her doll to the

family cabin. Her family likes it.

Details

Read the paragraph carefully. Find the details that tell about the topic.

Order of responses may vary.

    Molly and Henry live on the frontier. There are lots of fields and open spaces near their house. It is not crowded like a city. Their school is very close to their house. They can walk wherever they please because it is very safe where they live. Sometimes they see wild animals roaming through the fields. Molly and Henry love living in their frontier home.

Topic: Frontier

Detail: _____ fields nearby _____

Detail: _____ not crowded _____

Detail: _____ school nearby _____

Detail: _____ safe _____

Detail: _____ animals roam through the fields _____

Harcourt

Fluency Builder

beautiful	air	forming
nutrition	different	short
protects	flowers	for
ripens	grow	corn
streams	past	thorns
	plant	horses
	seed	
	tall	
	the	

1. The sunflowers / in the garden / will grow tall.

2. Water from the streams, / together with air and light, / will help the seeds / become flowers.

3. The seed / travels past the thorns / and the horses.

4. The pod ripens / and becomes corn.

5. There are seeds forming / on the pod.

6. The pod protects / the seeds.

7. Leaves make nutrition / for the plant.

8. Different kinds of flowers / are grown / in the garden.

A Day in the Life of a Seed

Look at the picture. Then do what the sentences tell you.

1. Bob, Cora, and Tim are on the team in the red shorts. Make their shorts red.

2. Peg, Mort, and Greg are on the team in the black shorts. Make Greg's shorts black.

3. Tim wants to score more runs. Give him a bat.

4. The team in the red shorts scored four runs. Put a four in the score box.

5. Greg is not playing the right sport. Put an X on his club.

Now circle the words above that have *or, ore,* and *our.*

Harcourt

A Day in the Life of a Seed

Complete the sentences with words from the box to tell what happens in "A Day in the Life of a Seed."

sprout	plant	soil	flowers	roots

1. The garden has lots of tall, yellow ___flowers___.

2. A rabbit pulls up grass. The seed falls to the ___soil___.

3. The seed will start to ___sprout___.

4. First, ___roots___ will form and go down into the soil.

5. Soon it becomes a tall ___plant___.

Write what you liked best about the story. Use as many words from the box as you can.

Responses will vary. _____

_____

_____

_____

Reading Diagrams

Read the diagram. Then use the labels to fill in the blanks.

1. This is the outside of the watermelon. _____*rind*_____.

2. These are found inside the watermelon. _____*seeds*_____.

3. This is attached to the watermelon. _____*vine*_____.

4. The vine grows out of this. _____*soil*_____.

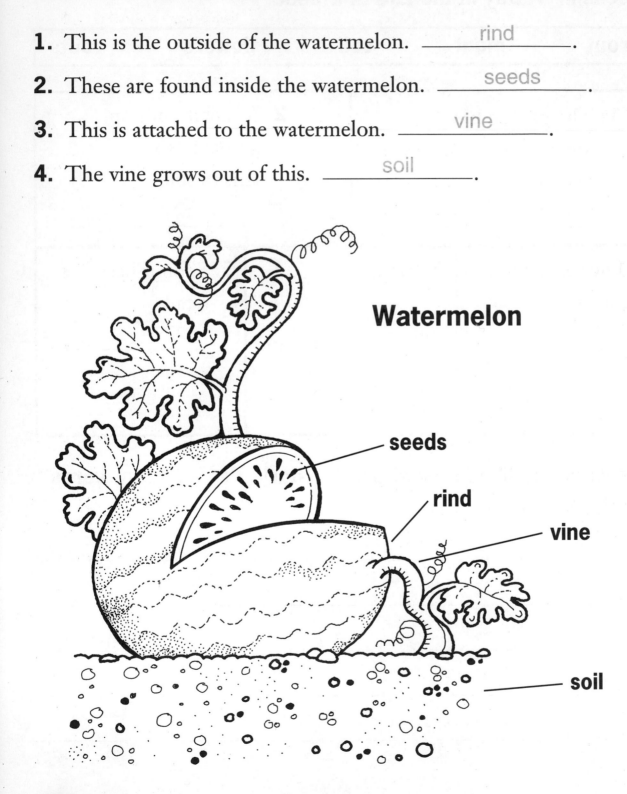

Watermelon

seeds

rind

vine

soil

Harcourt

Fluency Builder

discover	tree	her
energy	sun	weather
forecast	winds	uncurl
shed	winter	birds
source	bark	chirp
	little	perfect
	rabbit	turn
	family	

1. All summer, / the tree's leaves / take energy from the sun.

2. The cold winds / forecast winter weather.

3. Birds discover / the bugs / on the bark / of the tree.

4. The birds chirp and sleep / in the branches / of the tree.

5. In the spring / new little leaves uncurl / and turn / to the sun.

6. The log is / the perfect spot / for the mother rabbit / and her family.

7. The tree will shed / its bark.

8. A tree is / a source of life / to many living things.

The Old Tree

Read the story. Circle the words with *er*, *ir*, or *ur*.

A (bird) and a (turtle) met one day. "I can (surf!)" the (turtle) said.

"Well, I can fly," said the (bird). "Let's go up to my (perch)."

"Let's go (surfing)," said the (turtle). "No thanks," said the (bird). "I do not want to (surf). I will get my (shirt) wet."

"As you like," said the (turtle). "Now, will you get me back on (firm) ground? This (perch) is too far up for a (turtle)."

Circle the word to complete each sentence. Write it on the line.

1. A _____bird_____ and a turtle met one day.
   third **(bird)** **perfect**

2. The bird took the turtle to its _____perch_____ .
   surf **(perch)** **turn**

3. The bird did not want to get its _____shirt_____ wet.
   (shirt) **perch** **dirt**

4. The turtle wanted to get back on _____firm_____ ground.
   (firm) **term** **first**

Harcourt

Name _____

The Old Tree

Fill in the first two parts of the chart before you read the story.

What I Know	What I Want to Know	What I Learned

After you read, answer these questions. Then, in the third part of the chart, write new facts you learned.

1. What happens to the bark on a tree as it grows older and

   weaker? _____ The tree sheds its bark. _____

2. How do animals use dead tree parts such as empty logs?

   _____ Logs provide homes for animals. _____

3. What living thing can grow on a log?

   _____ Moss, a very small plant, can grow on a log. _____

Harcourt

Fact and Fiction

Read the description of each book. Look carefully at each book title on the book cover. Write *Fact* or *Fiction* on the lines.

Fact

Fiction

This book gives step-by-step directions for building the perfect campfire.

This book tells how a family of bunnies plans a surprise party for their best friend.

Fact

This book tells all about a second grade field trip to pick apples in an orchard. It includes photos.

Harcourt

Fluency Builder

beneath	look	sounds
knelt	all	ground
relay race	were	down
shimmered	over	sprouts
snug	good	now
wrinkled	made	proud
		pounded
		tower

1. Mr. Carver and Ben / were wrinkled all over.

2. The seeds / were snug / in the soil.

3. Ben / knelt down / on the ground / to look at the sprouts.

4. The sun / pounded down / on the sprouts.

5. The carrot sprouts shimmered / in the heat.

6. Ben made a tower / of carrots.

7. They / were very proud / of their garden.

8. Now / watermelon sounds good / to Ben and Mr. Carver.

Harcourt

Name _____

Mr. Carver's Carrots

Read the story. Circle all the words with the vowel sound you hear in *cow* and *found*.

At the Farm

Beth has a farm. Color her barn red. Color her (house) (brown). Beth has four (cows) and a cat called (Clown). (Clown) likes to run (around).

(Now) Beth is (plowing) the (ground). (Clown) has (found) a (mouse). The (mouse) is (about) to fall (down)!

Now write a word with *ou* or *ow* to complete each sentence.

1. Beth's house is _____ brown _____.

2. Beth has a cat and four _____ cows _____.

3. Now Beth is plowing the _____ ground _____.

4. The cat has _____ found _____ a mouse.

5. The mouse is about to fall _____ down _____.

Mr. Carver's Carrots

These events are from "Mr. Carver's Carrots." They are out of order. Put a number in front of each one to show the right order.

_4_   Mr. Carver and Ben munched on carrots.

_2_   Sprouts came up after a storm.

_3_   Mr. Carver and Ben pulled the carrots out of the ground.

_1_   Ben put carrot seeds under the soil.

Now write the events in order. Put each one next to its number.

1. Ben put carrot seeds under the soil. _____

_____

2. Sprouts came up after a storm. _____

_____

3. Mr. Carver and Ben pulled the carrots out of the ground. ___

_____

4. Mr. Carver and Ben munched on carrots. _____

_____

Harcourt

Make Inferences

Read the paragraph. Complete the sentence to make an inference. Write three clues that helped you make the inference.

Tom's alarm clock rang at 6 A.M. He jumped out of bed and dressed. He went to the back door, put on his rubber boots, and grabbed the milk pail. He could hear the cows in the barn. "I'm coming! I'm coming!" he called as he ran toward the barn.

Inference: Tom is going to milk the cows.

Clue: grabbed the milk pail

Clue: cows making noise

Clue: running towards barn

Harcourt

Fluency Builder

boasted	rabbit	shame
crept	fox	ate
crown	mouse	late
village	into	rake
vines	many	spade
	work	gate
	again	came
	from	

1. Miss Owl wins / the village's Best Melon Contest / all the time.

2. It's a shame / the leaves are small / and withered / on the tangled vines.

3. Kit Fox, / Pocket Mouse, / and Jack Rabbit / met at the gate / and crept / into the garden.

4. With a spade and a rake / they worked late.

5. They came / many evenings / to work in the garden.

6. "This is my best crop / ever," / boasted Miss Owl.

7. Everyone agreed / that she was sure / to win the crown / again this year.

8. They all ate / fresh watermelon / from the garden.

Miss Owl's Secret

Circle and write the word that makes the sentence tell about the picture.

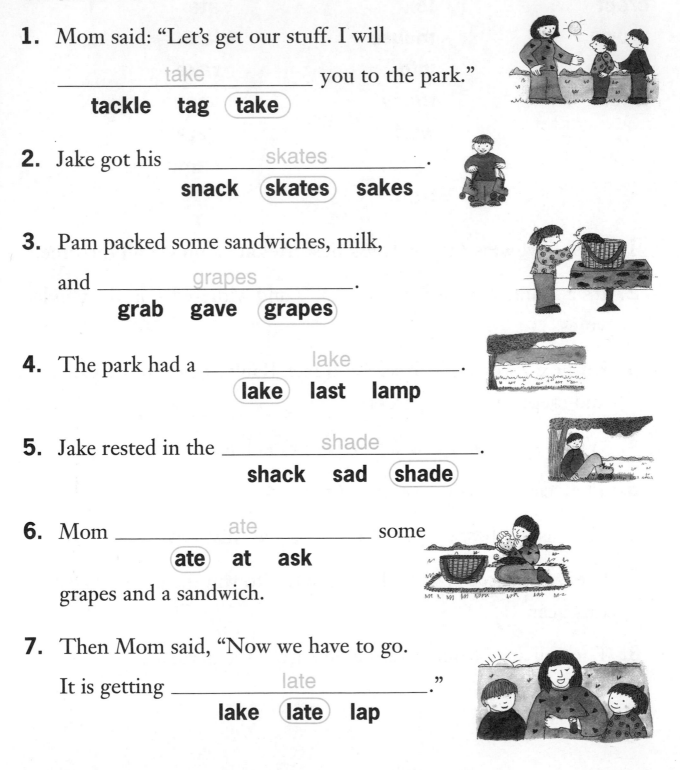

1. Mom said: "Let's get our stuff. I will

   _____ take _____ you to the park."

   tackle   tag   (take)

2. Jake got his _____ skates _____ .

   snack   (skates)   sakes

3. Pam packed some sandwiches, milk,

   and _____ grapes _____ .

   grab   gave   (grapes)

4. The park had a _____ lake _____ .

   (lake)   last   lamp

5. Jake rested in the _____ shade _____ .

   shack   sad   (shade)

6. Mom _____ ate _____ some

   (ate)   at   ask

   grapes and a sandwich.

7. Then Mom said, "Now we have to go.

   It is getting _____ late _____ ."

   lake   (late)   lap

Harcourt

Name _____

Miss Owl's Secret

Choose the word from the box that best completes each sentence. Write it on the line.

messy	crown	watermelon	night	dark

1. Miss Owl grew this _____watermelon_____ in her garden.

2. In the beginning, Miss Owl's garden was _____messy_____.

3. The animals worked in the garden at _____night_____.

4. The winner of the contest would get a _____crown_____.

5. Miss Owl can see in the _____dark_____.

Write why Miss Owl's friends wanted to help her by cleaning the garden.

Accept reasonable responses.

_____

_____

_____

Harcourt

Predict Outcomes

Read the story. Look for clues that help you predict what will happen at the end. Write your prediction and three clues that helped you.

Miss Gale's birthday was soon. Her class wanted to surprise her. At recess one day, they made plans. They knew she loved homemade things. She really liked drawings. The only way to keep it a surprise was to make a gift at recess. Michael said he would bring crayons. Mindy said she would bring art paper.

Predicted Outcome:
The children will make a birthday card at recess.

Clue:	Clue:	Clue:
Possible response:	Possible response:	Possible response:
Teacher's birthday is soon.	She likes drawings.	Children bring crayons and paper.

Harcourt

Fluency Builder

boring	game	Rose
ducked	fish	Duke
sense	want	close
suppose	play	doze
tractor	doesn't	Jerome
	someone	froze
	starts	dunes
	once	

1. Rose and Jerome / played a fishing game / on the porch.

2. Jerome did not want / to play / because the game / was boring.

3. I suppose / Rose doesn't like it / when Jerome starts / to doze.

4. There was / someone standing / by the dunes.

5. Jerome froze / and ducked down / next to Duke.

6. Once, / the farmer let / the children sit / on his tractor.

7. It did not make sense / to throw back / all the fish.

8. They walked / to the store / before it could close.

Harcourt

Name

The Not-So-Boring Night

Circle and write the word that makes the sentence tell about the picture.

1. Last summer, Jane rode a

_____mule_____ on a camping trip.

mug (mule) mop

2. Jane, Mom, and Dad rode up a

_____slope_____ to a lake.

(slope) cube stop

3. Jane used a _____pole_____

cute pot (pole)

to catch some fish.

4. Her dad found a red _____rose_____ .

run (rose) rock

5. The rose made his _____nose_____ itch.

not (nose) note

6. Mom dug a _____hole_____

hot (hole) hug

and put some stones around it.

7. Jane saw funny shapes in the

_____smoke_____ .

mule small (smoke)

8. When it got dark, the stars _____shone_____

(shone) spoke song

down on the camp.

Harcourt

Name _____

The Not-So-Boring Night

These events are from "The Not-So-Boring Night." They are out of order. Put a number in front of each one to show the right order.

_____2_____ The farmer was throwing back the fish he got.

_____4_____ Jerome said he liked the fishing game.

_____1_____ Duke and Jerome went for a walk.

_____3_____ Rose woke Jerome up.

Now write each event in the order it happened. Put each one next to an X. Then write other story events in order on the blank lines.

Jerome and Rose played a fishing game.
_____

[X] Duke and Jerome went for a walk.
_____

[X] The farmer was throwing back the fish he got.
_____

He told Jerome about his fishing game.
_____

[X] Rose woke Jerome up.
_____

[X] Jerome said he liked the fishing game.
_____

Name _____

Cause and Effect

Read the story.

The Boring Day

It was raining hard, and I could not go outside. I was bored.
I could not play cards, because my sister Lynn did not want to play
cards. She was baking a cake. When the cake was done, we could not
eat it. Our dog ate the whole thing! Possible responses are given.

Write three causes and three effects from the story.

Cause		Effect
It was raining hard.	→	I could not go outside.
My sister Lynn did not want to play cards.	→	I could not play cards.
Our dog ate the whole cake.	→	We could not eat the cake.

Harcourt

Fluency Builder

captured	hat	time
imagination	over	fine
manners	says	like
matador	train	tied
plains	my	lined
relax	were	
vacation	new	
	find	

1. On my vacation, / I met a matador.

2. In my imagination, / I made up a train / that rode / over the plains.

3. Don't let your imagination be captured— / relax, / let it rest.

4. My aunt says / that my manners / are fine.

5. We tied horns / on my hat.

6. There were / cowboys lined up / by the barbed wire.

7. It is time / for the matador / to find a new job.

8. He would like / to be a farmer.

Harcourt

The Matador and Me

Write the word that best completes each sentence.

| hike | kite | pies | stripes | tie | shines | rides |

1. Todd likes to play with his
_____kite_____.

2. Jane _____rides_____
her bike to the lake.

3. I see nine _____pies_____
in the kitchen.

4. Tim and Mike went for a
_____hike_____ up a hill.

5. Dom stops to _____tie_____
his shoelaces.

6. Dave wore a shirt with black
_____stripes_____.

7. The sun _____shines_____
on the vines.

The Matador and Me

Complete the puzzle using the words in the box. The answer for 2 Down has been done for you.

| parents | cowboys | aunt | train | instead | clothes |

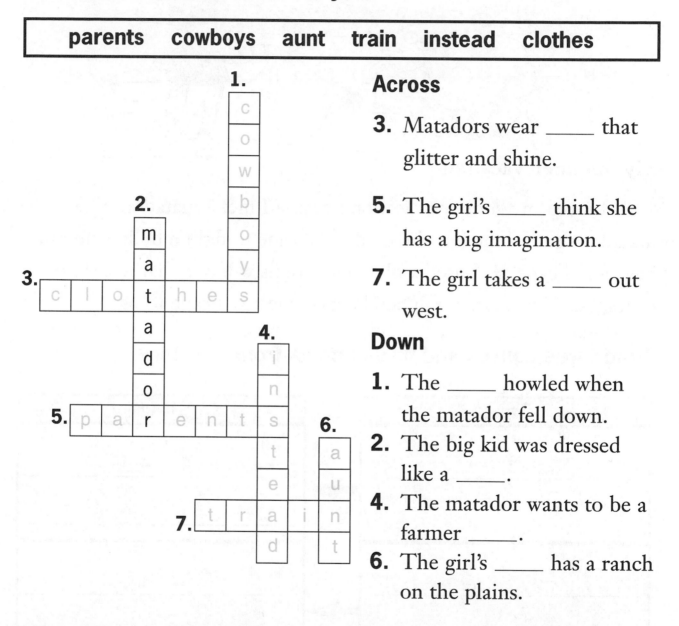

Across

3. Matadors wear _____ that glitter and shine.

5. The girl's _____ think she has a big imagination.

7. The girl takes a _____ out west.

Down

1. The _____ howled when the matador fell down.

2. The big kid was dressed like a _____.

4. The matador wants to be a farmer _____.

6. The girl's _____ has a ranch on the plains.

Write about your favorite part of the story. Use as many words from the box as you can.

Responses will vary.

_____

_____

_____

Harcourt

Name

Cause and Effect

Read the story.

My Summer Vacation

    I loved my summer vacation because I met a matador. The matador showed me how he used a red cape to fight a bull. I did not have a red cape, so I used a blue one. "Bulls will not charge at blue capes," said the matador. Then he gave me a red cape to use.

Write three causes and three effects from the story.

Cause		Effect
I met a matador.	→	I loved my summer vacation.
I did not have a red cape.	→	I used a blue one.
Bulls will not charge at blue capes.	→	The matador gave me a red cape to use.

Harcourt

Fluency Builder

details	**feed**	**Neal**
disappoint	**comes**	**seal**
forcibly	**really**	**beach**
information	**full**	**meet**
oceans	**well**	**each**
stroke		**teaches**
		seems
		real
		sleek

1. Neal meets / the seal / each weekend / on the beach.

2. Each time / they meet, / Mr. Whiskers teaches Neal / many details about seals.

3. He uses / his flippers forcibly / to reach / his top speed.

4. Oceans are full / of lots of animals / who feed on fish.

5. It seems / like the seal / talks to Neal, / but he really / does not.

6. Neal will stroke / Mr. Whiskers's back / for doing so well.

7. When Mr. Whiskers comes out / of the water, / he is so sleek!

8. Neal is disappointed / that his parents / do not think / Mr. Whiskers is real.

Mr. Whiskers

Fill in the oval in front of the sentence that tells about the picture best.

1
- ⬭ The cat is sleeping.
- ⬭ Chen is eating beets.
- ⬭ Chen is feeding her pet.

2
- ⬭ Fred and Kent have no sheets.
- ⬭ I see three beds.
- ⬭ Fred is dreaming of sheep.

3
- ⬭ Tom is sleeping on the beach.
- ⬭ A seal is swimming in the deep sea.
- ⬭ Meg has sneakers on her feet.

4
- ⬭ The sheep are near a tree.
- ⬭ I see three sheep and a bee.
- ⬭ The sheep are eating beans.

5
- ⬭ Ron is feeding the birds.
- ⬭ Three cats are in a tree.
- ⬭ Three birds in a tree want to eat.

6
- ⬭ I see bees in that tree.
- ⬭ There is one leaf left on that tree.
- ⬭ The leaf fell in the street.

Harcourt

Mr. Whiskers

Neal tells a lot about Mr. Whiskers. Write *first*, *next*, or *last* under each picture to show when Neal tells about each thing.

next _____   last _____   first _____

Complete each sentence so it tells about the story. Choose from the words in dark type.

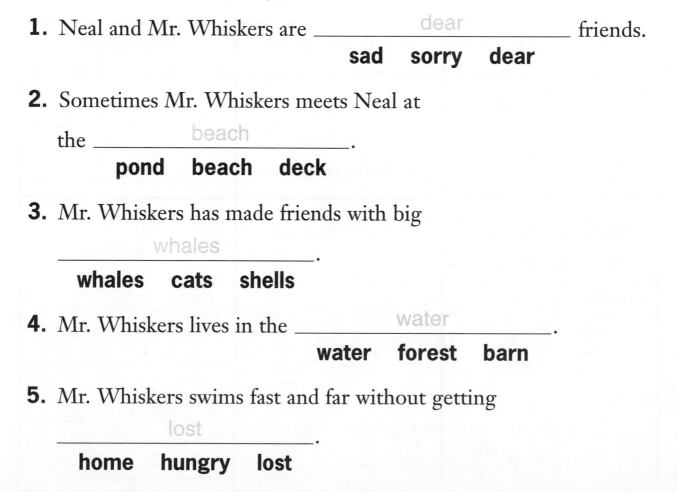

1. Neal and Mr. Whiskers are _____ dear _____ friends.

sad   sorry   dear

2. Sometimes Mr. Whiskers meets Neal at

the _____ beach _____.

pond   beach   deck

3. Mr. Whiskers has made friends with big

_____ whales _____.

whales   cats   shells

4. Mr. Whiskers lives in the _____ water _____.

water   forest   barn

5. Mr. Whiskers swims fast and far without getting

_____ lost _____.

home   hungry   lost

Harcourt

Make Inferences

Read the story. Then fill in the chart to make inferences.

Ms. Green

My name is Carla. This is Ms. Green, my turtle friend. I live in a house. Ms. Green lives in a pond. Ms. Green likes to eat flies, so I always bring her some for breakfast. Then Ms. Green teaches me about all the animals in the pond. My parents have never seen Ms. Green. I don't think my parents believe me when I talk about all the things Ms. Green tells me.

Clues from the Story	What We Know	Inference
Carla feeds Ms. Green	People who have pets should take good care of them.	Carla would make a good pet owner.
Carla's parents have never seen Ms. Green	Turtles do not talk.	Ms. Green does not really teach Carla about all the animals in the pond.

Harcourt

Fluency Builder

admired	not	Jules
fussed	after	fruit
haze	bed	tune
mimicked	made	flute
notice	bag	Sue
pale	play	clue
	you	blue

1. Jules was / the first to notice / that Mrs. Lee / was not at home.

2. There was a haze / the morning / after the rainstorm.

3. The nurse fussed / with the blue sheets / on the bed.

4. Mrs. Lee looked / a little pale.

5. The children had made / drawings for Mrs. Lee.

6. Jules mimicked Sue / playing a tune / on the flute.

7. The tape played / the sound / of fruit dropping / into a bag.

8. Jules gave / Mrs. Lee the clue, / "It is something / you can eat."

Harcourt

Sounds All Around

Write the word from the box that best completes each sentence.

| bluebird | flute | glue | fruit | suit | ruler |

1. Emily is playing a tune on her _____flute_____.

2. I see _____fruit_____ in that basket.

3. The _____bluebird_____ sings for Sue.

4. Sam has on a black _____suit_____.

5. The _____ruler_____ helps Marta draw a line.

6. Gunther uses _____glue_____ to make a model plane.

Harcourt

Sounds All Around

These events are from "Sounds All Around." They are out of order. Put a number in front of each one to show the right order.

___1___ Mr. Jones draws on the sidewalk.

___3___ Jules thinks of a plan.

___4___ Jules plays a tape for Mrs. Lee.

___2___ The rain makes a mess of the chalk drawings.

Now write each event next to an X in the order it happened. Fill in the other lines by telling what else happened in the story. Possible responses are shown.

Jules asks where Mrs. Lee is.

_____

Jules feels sad that Mrs. Lee is sick.

_____

[X] Mr. Jones draws on the sidewalk.

_____

[X] The rain makes a mess of the chalk drawings.

_____

[X] Jules thinks of a plan.

_____

Jules and his mom visit Mrs. Lee.

_____

Jules gives Mrs. Lee a big bag of presents.

_____

[X] Jules plays a tape for Mrs. Lee.

_____

Mrs. Lee draws a rainbow for her friends.

_____

Harcourt

Antonyms

Read the story. Then write an antonym, a word with an opposite meaning, for the words in the chart.

Sounds on My Street

There are a lot of nice sounds on my street. I hear children laughing. I hear birds singing a cheerful song. Sometimes I hear the ice cream truck playing its happy tune. Once in a while, there are loud sounds on my street. Sometimes I hear dump trucks. Sometimes I hear thunder from up in the sky.

Word from Story:	Antonym:
nice	awful
laughing	crying
cheerful	sad
happy	unhappy
loud	soft
up	down

Harcourt

Fluency Builder

flippers	sun	bay
hatch	out	may
miserable	their	plain
slippery	these	wait
waddled	would	lay
horizon	where	play
	little	raise

1. The sun sits low / on the horizon.

2. Little blue penguins / waddled out of the bay.

3. The penguins may wave / their flippers / to greet their mate.

4. Most penguins live / where they can play / on slippery ice slides.

5. These birds / would be miserable / where it is always cold.

6. In the summer / they lay / their eggs / and raise their chicks.

7. They wait / about one month / for their eggs / to hatch.

8. The chicks are covered / with plain, / dark down.

Little Blue Penguins

Read the story, and circle all the words with *ai* or *ay*.

One day Gail, her dad, and her dog Brain went for a hike. Brain started to bark. "Brain, are you barking at the snail on that log?" Gail asked. Brain barked some more. "Are you barking at the jay in that

tree?" she asked. Brain barked some more. "Are you barking at the ball on the trail?" Brain wagged his tail. Gail said, "I see! You want to play with that ball. Let's go!"

Choose from the words you circled to finish each sentence.

1. _____Brain_____ is the name of Gail's dog.

2. Gail asks Brain if he is barking at a _____snail_____ on a log.

3. Gail asks Brain if he is barking at a _____jay_____ in a tree.

4. Brain is barking at a ball on the _____trail_____.

5. Gail knows this after Brain wags his _____tail_____.

6. Gail knows Brain wants to _____play_____ with the ball.

Harcourt

Little Blue Penguins

Complete the sentences with words from the box to tell what happens in "Little Blue Penguins."

flippers	eggs	underground nests
krill	Antarctica	smallest

Little blue penguins live in _____underground nests_____.

Tunnels keep their _____eggs_____ safe.

Little blue penguins are the _____smallest_____ penguins.

Little blue penguins use their wings as _____flippers_____.

Little blue penguins do not live in _____Antarctica_____.

Little blue penguins eat sea animals called _____krill_____.

Write what you liked best about little blue penguins.

_____Responses will vary._____

_____

Harcourt

Fact and Fiction

Read the story. Then use the story to fill in two details that are facts and two details that are fiction. Then tell how you made your choices.

Rita the Robin

One day, Rita the Robin decided she needed a bigger home. Robins make their homes in nests made of twigs. "I will build a big nest made of bricks," said Rita. "But first, I need to eat breakfast." In the ground below, there were a lot of tasty worms. Robins like to eat worms.

Fact: _Robins make their_

homes in nests made of twigs.

Fact: _Robins like to eat worms._

_____

How I Know: _I can read a_

book to find out where robins

make their homes and what

they eat.

Fiction: _Rita the Robin decided_

she needed a bigger home.

Fiction: _"I will build a big nest_

made of bricks," said Rita.

How I Know: _Robins do not_

decide things. Robins cannot

talk or build nests out of

bricks.

Harcourt

Fluency Builder

caused	day	Jo
clasp	over	shiny
confused	find	we
cornered	because	secret
objects	snow	gold
removes	day	
typical	look	
	your	

1. A snow day is not / a typical day / for Lee and Jo.

2. What caused / the blocks / to be knocked over?

3. They look for clues / to find the missing objects.

4. Mom is confused / because the clasp / on her key ring / is broken.

5. A shiny gold key / will be easy / to spot.

6. We will remove / the lumps / from your bed, / Wags.

7. They have / Wags cornered.

8. Does Wags have / a secret hiding place / of his own?

Name _____

A Secret Place

Read the story.

Di sells watches and clocks. This morning, she sold a clock.

At lunchtime, she sold a gold watch.

At six, it was time to go. It was cold outside. Di put on a coat.

Di closed the blinds. Then she went home.

Write the word that best completes each sentence.

1. _____ Di _____ works in a store.

   Di   Coco   Matt

2. First, she _____ sold _____ a clock.

   song   sold   so

3. Then _____ she _____ sold a gold watch.

   I   she   we

4. She put on a coat because it was _____ cold _____.

   cold   clock   fold

5. At six, she closed the _____ blinds _____.

   bins   grinds   blinds

Harcourt

Name _____

A Secret Place

Complete the chart with words from the box to tell what happened in "A Secret Place."

small	missing	chief	key	shiny	clues

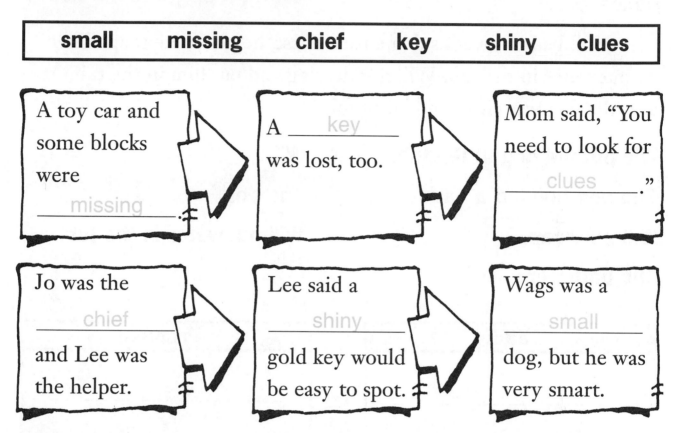

A toy car and some blocks were _____missing_____.

A ___key___ was lost, too.

Mom said, "You need to look for _____clues_____."

Jo was the _____chief_____ and Lee was the helper.

Lee said a _____shiny_____ gold key would be easy to spot.

Wags was a _____small_____ dog, but he was very smart.

Answer these questions to tell about the rest of the story.

1. What were the missing things? toy car, blocks, key

_____

2. Who had the missing things? Wags the dog

3. Who found the missing things? Jo and Lee

4. Think of another way the family could have found the missing things. Write it here. Responses may vary.

_____

Narrative Elements

Read the story and copy the narrative elements in the correct boxes.

Will had to give his dog a bath. First, he got some soap. Then he put water in the tub. Will got the dog and put him in the tub. At last, the dog was clean and beautiful.

Will put the dog in the tub.   **Will**

The dog needed a bath.   **The dog**

Will got soap.   **Will put water in the tub.**

The bathroom

Setting	Problem
The bathroom	The dog needed a bath.

Characters	Events
Will the dog	Will got soap. Will put water in the tub.

How Problem is Solved
Will put the dog in the tub.

Fluency Builder

addresses	started	sky
clerk	know	Myles
grown	think	Clyde
honor	tried	Pryor
pour	was	fly
route	into	July
	play	spy

1. Myles lives / in the sky-blue house / next to Ms. Pryor, / the town clerk.

2. In July / mail started / to pour / into the children's mailboxes.

3. Who would know / all of their addresses?

4. Myles tried / to think / like a spy.

5. The mail was not coming / on the mail route.

6. A grown person / was sneaking / the mail / into the mailboxes.

7. Myles planned / a birthday party / in honor / of Mr. Clyde.

8. They will play games / and fly kites!

Harcourt

Hello from Here

Write the word that completes each sentence best.

by	fly	dry	Why	tries	sky	cries	shy

1. Little Robin sees birds up in the ____sky____.

2. He wants to ____fly____ in the sky, too.

3. ____Why____ is flying so hard?

4. Little Robin feels a little bit ____shy____.

5. Now he is wet, but he wants to be ____dry____.

6. Little Robin ____cries____ hard.

7. He ____tries____ to fly again.

8. Now Little Robin can fly all ____by____ himself!

Harcourt

Name

Hello from Here

Write a word to complete the sentences about the story. Choose from the words in dark type.

1. Mr. Clyde had no _____grandchildren_____.

        mailbox   car   grandchildren

2. Mr. Clyde gave the kids a big _____surprise_____.

        surprise   cake   party

3. One boy hid by a _____mailbox_____ to find out who sent the postcards.   **car   mailbox   house**

4. He saw Mr. Clyde coming up the _____street_____.

        street   steps   ramp

5. Mr. Clyde had waited _____years_____ to try sky diving.

        what   days   years

6. The kids had a _____party_____ for Mr. Clyde.

        card   kite   party

Write answers to these questions.

7. What clue did the boy use to find out who was sending the cards?

There were no stamps on the cards.

8. Why did the boy send cards to the kids on his street?

He invited them to a party for Mr. Clyde.

Harcourt

Compare and Contrast

Read the stories. Then fill in the diagram to show how the stories are alike and different.

Story 1

The kittens were in their basket. Their mother was off looking for food. One kitten saw some yarn on the floor. He wanted to get it. He left the basket. His sisters came, too. They played with the ball of yarn for a long time. When their mother came back, they were all asleep in the basket. They had played hard.

Story 2

Jason was in his yard. He was playing ball. He hit the ball with his bat. The ball went up in the sky. His mother came to catch it. Jason and his mother played together for a long time. They had a lot of fun. When they were done, Jason went to sleep. It had been a long day.

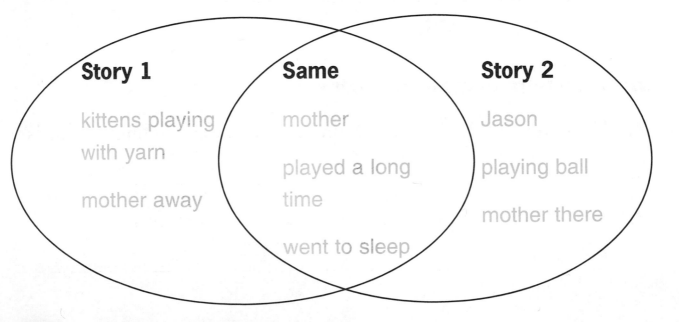

Story 1

kittens playing with yarn

mother away

Same

mother

played a long time

went to sleep

Story 2

Jason

playing ball

mother there

Harcourt

Fluency Builder

appeared	liked	Dwight
conductor	find	right
created	would	fright
imitated	side	night
rhythm	dad	high
startled	game	delighted
	new	
	his	

1. Dwight liked to find / new ways / to make his rhythm / sound better.

2. He would try / to get / just the right sound.

3. The loud sound / startled the children nearby.

4. Linda appeared / by his side / and said, / "You gave me / such a fright!"

5. Jon imitated / a trumpet player.

6. Dwight's dad created / a steel drum / in his workshop.

7. The conductor lifted his arms high, / and Dwight / delighted the crowd.

8. He played / "The Star-Spangled Banner" / at the game Saturday night.

The Music Maker

Write the word that makes the sentence tell about the picture.

1. "Let's take a walk to the _____ lighthouse _____," said Mom.

   nightshirt　　**nighttime**　　**lighthouse**

2. "How will we find the path at _____ night _____?" asked Tim.

   fight　　**night**　　**tight**

3. "We will use a _____ flashlight _____," Mom replied.

   flashlight　　**lightning**　　**night**

4. The lighthouse sits _____ high _____ up on a cliff.

   sight　　**hide**　　**high**

5. It has a big _____ light _____ at the top.

   flight　　**light**　　**like**

6. The light is very _____ bright _____.

   bride　　**might**　　**bright**

7. The light shows ships the _____ right _____ way to go.

   ride　　**right**　　**rind**

8. Ann tells her mom, "I _____ might _____ work there someday."

   might　　**night**　　**light**

Harcourt

Name

The Music Maker

Write a word on each line. Complete the story strip to show the order of events in "The Music Maker."

Dwight put rubber bands on his _____sticks_____. **sticks** **drum**	First, Dwight drummed on his _____boxes_____. **bucket** **boxes**	Next, Dwight drummed on the _____bucket_____. **bucket** **basket**
When Dwight drummed on a _____garbage can_____, **garbage can** **box** he gave his friends a fright.	Dwight planned to play a tune at the _____game_____ **game** **show** on Saturday.	Linda said, "You can't play a _____tune_____ **rhythm** **tune** with a drum."
Dwight _____answered_____, **answered** **danced** "Yes, I can."	Dwight's dad _____made_____ **made** **bought** steel drums.	When he put the heated can in water, _____clouds_____ **drops** **clouds** of steam came up.

Harcourt

Multiple-meaning Words

A **multiple-meaning word** has more than one meaning. Read the words around it to find out which meaning makes sense.

Read the sentences. Decide which meaning is correct.

1. I will **plant** this tree.

   a. a green, growing thing

   (b.) to put into the ground

2. I will keep the **flies** off it.

   a. moves through the air

   (b.) small, black bugs

3. I will keep the **cold** off it.

   (a.) the opposite of heat

   b. a runny nose

4. I will give it to my dad as a **present**.

   (a.) gift

   b. right now

Harcourt

Fluency Builder

dappled	your	shiny
exhibitions	would	pony
landscape	work	risky
business	falls	dirty
ranch	have	dusty
thousands	their	silly
	horses	field

1. Would you trade / your shiny bike / for a dappled pony?

2. The rodeo is / an exhibition / of style and skill.

3. Many riders / in small rodeos / work on a ranch.

4. If a cowboy falls off of a bronco, / then he'll see the landscape / up close.

5. Ropers have to practice / their skill / thousands of times.

6. Riding a bull / is a risky business.

7. Silly clowns have / dirty, / dusty, / and dangerous work.

8. At the end of the rodeo, / horses can go out / to the field and graze.

Harcourt

Rodeo!

Complete each sentence with a word from the box.

chilly	sleepy	puppies	dirty
Fluffy	family	hungry	happy

1. Penny asks, "Mom, may I have
   one of the _____puppies_____?"

2. Mom asks, "Penny, will you feed the
   puppy when he is _____hungry_____?"

3. "Will you wash the puppy when
   he is _____dirty_____?"

4. "Will you walk the puppy when it
   is _____chilly_____ outside?"

5. "Will you play with the puppy at night
   when you are _____sleepy_____?"

6. Penny says, "Yes, Mom. The puppy will
   be very _____happy_____ with me."

7. Mom says, "Now the puppy is a part of our
   _____family_____. What will you call him?"

8. Penny says, "I will call him
   _____Fluffy_____!"

Rodeo!

Complete the puzzle with words from the box.

| horse | practice | rope | ride | birthday | style |

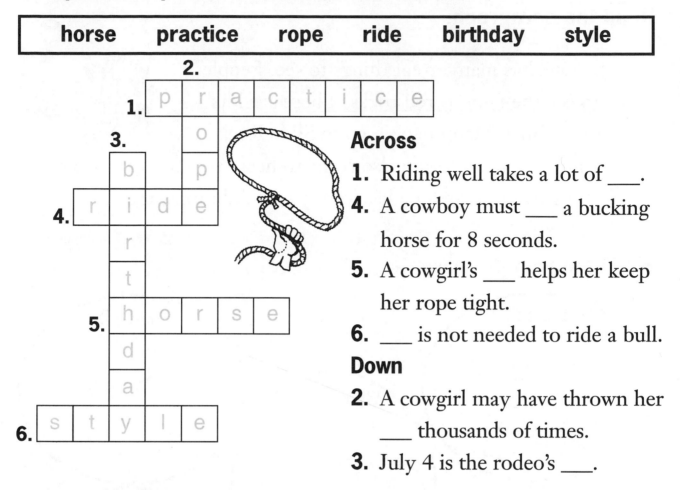

2.
1. p r a c t i c e
3. o
b p
4. r i d e
r
t
5. h o r s e
d
a
6. s t y l e

Across

1. Riding well takes a lot of ___.
4. A cowboy must ___ a bucking horse for 8 seconds.
5. A cowgirl's ___ helps her keep her rope tight.
6. ___ is not needed to ride a bull.

Down

2. A cowgirl may have thrown her ___ thousands of times.
3. July 4 is the rodeo's ___.

Write the completed clues on the lines below.

Riding well takes a lot of practice. _____

A cowboy must ride a bucking horse for 8 seconds. _____

A cowgirl's horse helps her keep her rope tight. _____

Style is not needed to ride a bull. _____

A cowgirl may have thrown her rope thousands of times. _____

July 4 is the rodeo's birthday. _____

_____

Summarize/Restate

Read the paragraph.

Sedona has many great things to see. People come to see the famous red rocks. There are lots of places to hike. Many people go to Slide Rock to play in the water. People also come to hear jazz. You can also ride in a hot-air balloon. Sedona has lots of art exhibitions, too.

Fill in the web. Possible responses are given.

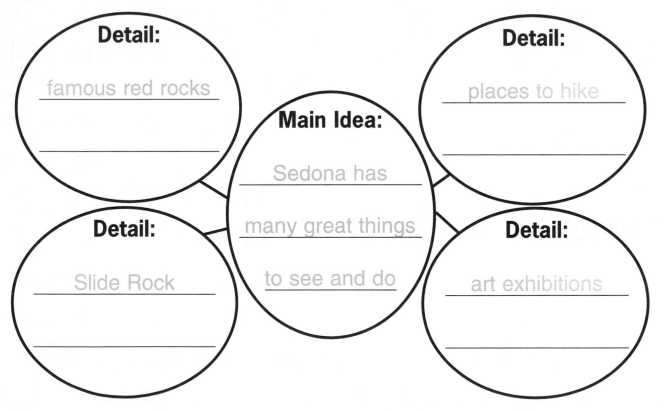

Detail:
famous red rocks

Detail:
places to hike

Main Idea:
Sedona has
many great things
to see and do

Detail:
Slide Rock

Detail:
art exhibitions

Use your web to write a summary on the lines below.

Responses may vary.

_____

_____

Harcourt

Fluency Builder

celebrations	with	roads
develop	Grandma	blowing
furious	all	showed
graceful	trucks	loaf
grocery store	store	grow
students	cake	glowed
	lion	
	when	

1. Chinese characters are made / with graceful brush strokes.

2. Of all the celebrations, / the Chinese New Year / is Grandma's favorite.

3. Chinatown's roads were noisy / with delivery trucks / and blowing horns.

4. Grandma showed Jimmy / how to shop for fruit / at the grocery store.

5. At the bakery / they bought a loaf, / sweets, / and a New Year's cake.

6. The kung fu students / were carrying / a furious-looking lion mask.

7. Grandma told Jimmy / that melon will help you / develop and grow.

8. Jimmy glowed / with happiness / when his parents arrived.

Happy New Year!

Fill in the oval in front of the sentence that tells about the picture.

1 ◯ Ron owns a white coat.

⬤ Ron rows a boat.

◯ Ron is throwing a snowball.

2 ⬤ The plant is slow to grow.

◯ Joan will eat some toast.

◯ I see a flower in the snow.

3 ◯ The bowl is round.

◯ Tam shows Rick her new soap.

⬤ Rick knows Tam owns a ball.

4 ◯ The coach is mowing the grass.

◯ A girl throws the coat.

⬤ Joan has scored a goal.

5 ◯ The log floats on a road.

⬤ Four toads sit in a row.

◯ I see three toads and a goat.

6 ⬤ The truck can tow a boat.

◯ A crow is on the truck.

◯ Joan and Bob will tow a bowl.

Harcourt

Happy New Year!

These events are from the story "Happy New Year!" They are out of order. Put a number in front of each one to show the right order.

_2_ Jimmy and Grandma went shopping.

_4_ Jimmy's mother and father came back early.

_1_ Jimmy and Grandma cleaned the apartment.

_3_ The family members began to arrive.

Answer these questions to tell about the rest of the story.

1. What did Jimmy and Grandma hang up in the apartment?

spring scrolls with graceful brush strokes

2. What did Jimmy and Grandma buy when they went shopping?

fruit, a loaf, sweets, cake

3. What did the kung fu students have?

a furious-looking lion mask

4. Why did Grandma set out chairs for Jimmy's parents?

It was an old custom to set out chairs for those who could

not be there.

Harcourt

Details

Read the paragraph.

Long ago in China there was a monster. Its name was Nian. He liked to scare people. The people did not like him. "Go pick on other monsters," they cried. Nian went away for a year. Then he came back. Some children were using fire-crackers. BANG! The noise scared Nian away. Now people always use firecrackers on Chinese New Year. They keep Nian away.

Write four details from the paragraph that tell about Nian.

Possible responses are given.

1. **Detail** _He liked to scare people._

2. **Detail** _People did not like him._

3. **Detail** _He went away for a year._

4. **Detail** _Firecrackers scared him away._

Harcourt

Fluency Builder

flock	wanted	look
glide	bird	book
harbor	over	cook
soared	rain	soon
swooping	down	
clouds	across	
window	would	
everyone	world	

1. Luke wanted / to glide / like a bird.

2. In his imagination / he soared / over the rain clouds.

3. June would join / a flock of birds / down at the harbor.

4. She would go swooping / across the wide / blue sea.

5. Soon / everyone would know / how to fly.

6. Sally would look / in her grandma's window.

7. Grandma would cook Sally / the best meal / in the world.

8. Sally would read / from her book / until her grandma / fell asleep.

Harcourt

If I Could Fly

Fill in the oval in front of the sentence that tells about the picture.

1 ◯ Sue put the ball in the pool.
   ⬭ The ball went in the hoop.
   ◯ Sue stood on the book.

2 ◯ The robin makes a loop.
   ◯ The bird is at the zoo.
   ⬭ The bird flies in front of the moon.

3 ⬭ Nate shook the fruit down.
   ◯ Nate waded in the brook.
   ◯ Nate stood on a stool.

4 ◯ Lew gives the book to Sue.
   ⬭ Lew has a new cookbook.
   ◯ Lew likes his new boots.

5 ◯ My boots are in that room.
   ◯ We will go to the pool soon.
   ⬭ There is a toolbox on the roof.

6 ◯ Dan looks for his blue shoe.
   ⬭ He cooks a good stew.
   ◯ The boy hooks a fish in the brook.

Harcourt

If I Could Fly

Read the clues. Then complete the puzzle with words from the box.

country	adventure	grandma	city	buildings	people

1. c i t y

2. a d v e n t u r e

3. b u i l d i n g s

4. g r a n d m a

5. p e o p l e

6. c o u n t r y

Across

3. Luke wanted to look into the windows of ____.

6. June said she wanted to go to a new ____.

Down

1. Luke wanted to go to a ____.

2. Luke told his friends he would have the best ____.

4. Sally said she wanted to visit her ____.

5. June said she wanted to find a place where ____ play all the time.

On another sheet of paper, write the completed clues. Write a number in front of each sentence to show the order of events in the story.

Make Inferences

Read the story. Then use clues from the story and what you know to make inferences about the girl in the story.

If No One Could See Me

My name is Sara. I like to play make-believe. Sometimes I pretend that no one can see me. If no one could see me, I would help people who were in trouble. For example, I would pick people up after they fell. They would be so surprised! Then I would let them see me, and we would laugh.

Story Clue: Sara likes to play make-believe.

What I Know: _People who like to play make-believe have_

good imaginations.

My Inference: _Sara has a good imagination._

Story Clue: Sara would help people who were in trouble.

What I Know: _People who help others are kind._

_____

My Inference: _Sara is a kind person._

Harcourt

Fluency Builder

connects	made	orange
distance	world	German
features	round	Germany
mapmaker	and	pages
peel	went	change
	trip	game
	between	
	through	
	your	

1. The mapmaker made / a globe round / to be a model / of the world.

2. If you could peel the globe / like an orange / and lay the strips flat, / then you would have / a world map.

3. A globe shows / land and water features.

4. The Atlantic Ocean connects / the continents / of South America / and Africa.

5. Pretend you went / on a trip / to a German village.

6. What is the distance / between your home / and Germany?

7. Look through the pages / of books / to find the answers.

8. How can you change / the rules of the game / to make it / even more fun?

Map Games

Read this story. Circle the words that have the g sound you hear in gem.

Gerry and Ginny

(Gerry) thinks this is a good day to be outside. He walks past the (hedge) to the (edge) of the river. He sits under a (giant) tree. (Gerry) looks at the sky. He feels a (gentle) wind.

(Ginny) thinks this is a good day to be inside. She thinks it is going to rain. She wants to play inside. She goes to the (gym) to play games.

Use some of the words you circled to complete each sentence.

1. Gerry sits by the _____ edge _____ of the river.

2. He is near a _____ giant _____ tree.

3. There is a _____ gentle _____ wind.

4. _____ Ginny _____ goes inside.

5. She wants to play games in the _____ gym _____.

Harcourt

Name _____

Map Games

Circle the word that best completes each sentence. Write it on the line.

1. You can use a

_____ globe _____

ball   orange   (globe)

to play map games.

2. A globe shows land and water

_____ features _____ .

continents (features) villages

3. The Atlantic Ocean

_____ connects _____

(connects)   peels   distances

the continents of South America and Africa.

4. You can guess the

_____ distance _____

feature   map   (distance)

from one place on the globe to another.

5. A globe is like a round _____ map _____ .

village   continent   (map)

On the lines below, write what you learned from the story.

Accept reasonable responses.

_____

_____

Name _____

Locate Information

Read the table of contents for an atlas. Then use the table of contents to answer the questions.

My Atlas
Table of Contents

Chapter 1: North America

Page 1...Map
Page 2...Mountain Ranges
Page 3...Rivers and Lakes
Page 4...Deserts
Page 5...People

Chapter 2: Africa

Page 6...Map
Page 7...Mountain Ranges
Page 8...Rivers and Lakes
Page 9...Deserts
Page 10...People

1. On which page would you find information about the

   Mississippi River in North America? _____ page 3 _____

2. Where would you find a picture of the continent of Africa?

   _____ page 6 _____

3. Which pages would help you compare and contrast the

   mountain ranges of North America and Africa?

   _____ pages 2 and 7 _____

4. Which page might tell you about where people work in Africa?

   _____ page 10 _____

Harcourt

 110 Grade 2 • Lesson 27/Focus Skill Review

Fluency Builder

cassette	you	joy
companions	want	point
luggage	ask	noise
relatives	help	join
sturdy	around	avoid
	too	toys
	lot	boys
	with	

1. Make a point / to call your relatives / before you visit.

2. You might want to ask / if a companion / can join you.

3. Pack sturdy clothes / and toys / in your luggage.

4. The boys offer to help / with the chores / around the house.

5. Avoid turning / your cassette player / too high.

6. Don't make / a lot of noise.

7. Make a point / of writing / a thank-you note.

8. Your relatives will remember / your visit / with joy!

When You Visit Relatives

Complete each sentence so it tells about the picture.

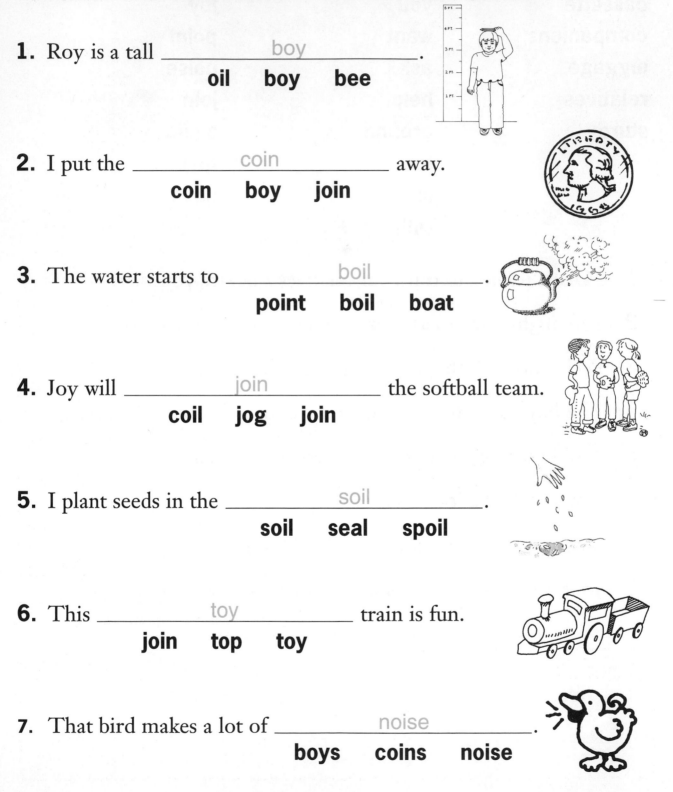

1. Roy is a tall _____ *boy* _____ .

          oil   boy   bee

2. I put the _____ *coin* _____ away.

        coin   boy   join

3. The water starts to _____ *boil* _____ .

        point   boil   boat

4. Joy will _____ *join* _____ the softball team.

        coil   jog   join

5. I plant seeds in the _____ *soil* _____ .

        soil   seal   spoil

6. This _____ *toy* _____ train is fun.

        join   top   toy

7. That bird makes a lot of _____ *noise* _____ .

        boys   coins   noise

Harcourt

When You Visit Relatives

Write *beginning*, *middle*, or *end* under each picture to show the order of events in "When You Visit Relatives."

middle   end   beginning

Now use the words in the gray boxes to answer the questions.
Possible responses are shown.

Beginning   `relatives   travel`

What does Ernest want to do? He wants to travel to visit

his relatives.

Middle   `bicycle   weather   forgets`

What is Ernest's trip like? He rides his bicycle. He forgets his

raincoat. The weather is bad, so he gets all wet.

What happens at his relatives' house?   `helps   broke`

Ernest helps with the chores. A dish broke.

End   `note   relatives`

What does Ernest remember to do at the end of his visit?

He writes a thank-you note to his relatives.

Harcourt

Author's Purpose

Write the author's purpose. Write three clues that helped you tell the author's purpose.

Here Comes Company!

   If you want to get ready for company, you should give yourself lots of time. First, you should clean your room. Then, you can prepare some nice snacks. Put the toys and the games you will want to play with your company in a neat pile. After that, you may want to take a bath and put on some nice clothes. Finally, wait for the doorbell to ring!

Author's Purpose:	To give information
Clue:	The story gives instructions for how to get ready for company.
Clue:	The steps are in time order.
Clue:	The information is not silly.

Harcourt

Fluency Builder

cozy	rain	caused
drifted	cave	crawled
fleet	past	hawk
launched	find	dawn
looming	would	paused
realized	were	saw
	from	yawned

1. Zelda yawned / when she reached / her cozy cave.

2. The rain caused / the water / to rise / in the cave.

3. Zelda crawled out / onto the ledge.

4. A bottle drifted past / in the waves.

5. Zelda realized / she would have / to find / a new home.

6. Dark clouds were looming / when Zelda launched herself / from the ledge.

7. Zelda flew / like a hawk / over a fleet / of sailboats.

8. Zelda paused / at dawn / when she saw / sand below.

Name _____

Zelda Moves to the Desert

Read the sentences, then do what they tell you.

1. Do you see the baby crawling? Color his shirt yellow.
2. Can you find the hawk? Draw a tree for it to perch on.
3. Color the lawn green.
4. Do you see someone yawning? Color her shirt blue.
5. Find the fawn and circle it. Color it brown.
6. Shauna has pasta with sauce for lunch. Color the sauce red.
7. Draw some clouds in the sky.
8. Can you see the dog? Color him black with white paws.

Circle the words with the vowel sound you hear in *saw*.

Harcourt

Name _____

Zelda Moves to the Desert

Complete the flowchart with words from the box to tell what happens in "Zelda Moves to the Desert."

| waves | bottle | sank | flooded | sail | mice |

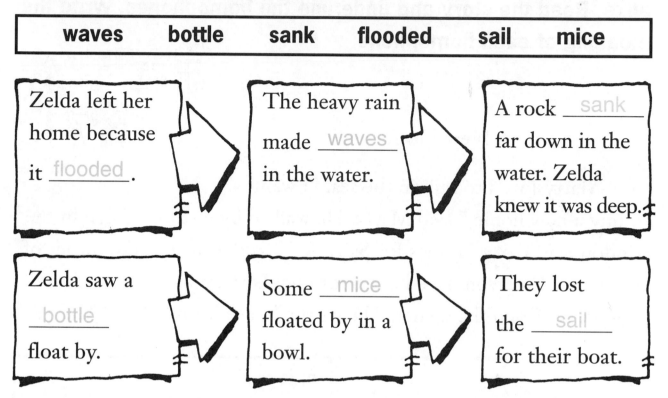

Zelda left her home because it _flooded_.

The heavy rain made _waves_ in the water.

A rock _sank_ far down in the water. Zelda knew it was deep.

Zelda saw a _bottle_ float by.

Some _mice_ floated by in a bowl.

They lost the _sail_ for their boat.

Answer these questions to tell about the rest of the story.

1. Where did Zelda fly first? _the forest_

2. Was that a good home for her? Explain your answer. _No, because it was too damp._

3. Where did Zelda fly next? _over the sea_

4. Where did Zelda find her new home? _in a cave in the desert_

_____

Harcourt

Homophones

Homophones are words that sound alike but are not spelled alike. Read the story and underline the homophones. Write the meaning of each homophone.

A New Home

Marty loved to <u>sail</u> on the <u>sea</u>. "I want to <u>buy</u> a new home," said Marty. He walked <u>by</u> a store. A sign in the window said Cozy Homes for <u>Sale</u>. "Hi," said Marty to the owner of the store. "I <u>see</u> you have homes for sale. Do you have a houseboat?" "Yes we do," said the owner. "That's the house for me!" said Marty.

sail	sale
to travel on water in a boat	selling something
sea	**see**
large body of water	to look at
buy	**by**
to spend money to get something	near

Harcourt

Fluency Builder

feat	who	city
heroine	her	celebrate
hospitality	came	cities
refused	from	decided
spectators	their	since
stood	around	chance
	world	center

1. Amelia Earhart / was a heroine / who accomplished / a great feat.

2. Amelia refused / to sit at home / in the city.

3. Soon flying became / the center / of Amelia's life.

4. Spectators came / from miles around / and stood / to celebrate Amelia's arrival.

5. Amelia thanked / the different cities / for their hospitality.

6. Amelia decided / to fly / all the way / around the world.

7. Hundreds of people / have looked / for the plane / ever since it disappeared.

8. Amelia took a chance / to fulfill her dreams.

Harcourt

An Amazing Feat

Read the story. Circle the words that have the c sound you hear in *city*.

The Race

Today is the bicycle race in Cedar City. The race goes in a big circle around Cash Park. Kim finds a space at the starting line. He ties his shoelaces. He puts on his nice new helmet. Then the race begins. The wind on Kim's face is cool. After the race, Kim drinks some juice. He didn't win, but he still celebrates with his mom and dad.

Choose from the words you circled to complete each sentence.

1. There is a bicycle _____race_____ today.

2. The race is in Cedar _____City_____.

3. The race goes in a big _____circle_____ around the park.

4. Kim feels the wind on his _____face_____.

5. He drinks _____juice_____ after the race.

6. He _____celebrates_____ with his mom and dad.

Harcourt

Name _____

An Amazing Feat

Complete the chart to tell about the story.

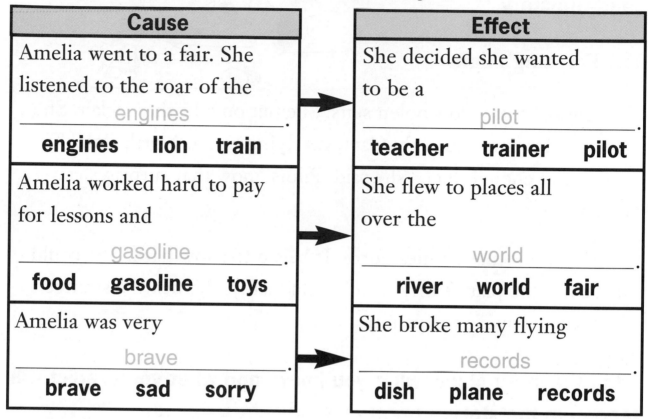

Cause	Effect
Amelia went to a fair. She listened to the roar of the ___engines___. **engines lion train**	She decided she wanted to be a ___pilot___. **teacher trainer pilot**
Amelia worked hard to pay for lessons and ___gasoline___. **food gasoline toys**	She flew to places all over the ___world___. **river world fair**
Amelia was very ___brave___. **brave sad sorry**	She broke many flying ___records___. **dish plane records**

Answer these questions to tell about the rest of the story.

1. What brave thing did Amelia want to do when she was 40?

She wanted to fly all the way around the world.

_____

2. What was her plane filled with? _____ gasoline _____

3. What happened to Amelia on this flight? Her plane

disappeared.

4. If you could meet Amelia Earhart, what would you ask her?

Responses will vary.

Harcourt

Predict Outcomes

Read the story.

The Freezing Flight

Cara put on two woolen suits. She put on a leather jacket. She needed to be warm enough. Cara was flying to the North Pole! "I hope I have enough fuel," she said. Pilots know that surprises can happen.

Cara flew many miles north. It began to snow hard. She could not see out the plane's tiny window. Suddenly, she heard a strange sound. It was inside the plane.

Fill in the story clues, what you know, and what you predict will happen in the story. Accept reasonable responses.

Story Clues	What I Know	My Prediction
Cara was flying to the North Pole.		
Cara heard a strange sound.		

Harcourt